For Merveille,

I hope you enjoy reading all about Mya and her family lunch!

I can't wait for you to read the other books!!

lots of love

Jeannelle xxx

AF471250

By Jeannelle Brew

Bryan House Publishing
Children's Books

Bryan House
Publishing

First Published in the United Kingdom by BRYAN HOUSE PUBLISHING
2017
The rights of Jeannelle Brew to be identified as the Author of the work has
been asserted by her in accordance with the Copyright, Design and Patents
Act 1988 ©

ISBN 978-0-9956017-5-8

Apart from any use permitted under UK Copyright law this publication
may only be reproduced, stored, or transmitted, in any form, or by any
means, with prior permission in writing of the publishers.

Edited by Jasmina Coric
Co-Edited by Hena Bryan
Book design by Jasmina Coric
Printed and bound in the UK by
IngramSpark

It was a crisp and cool Sunday afternoon; the leaves swayed and swished,
playing a game with the gentle wind.

A golden brown leaf would playfully rise and fall.
A dark green leaf would float, high and tall.
A deep orange leaf would lightly skid across the ground making a teeny
tiny sound.

'Look!' cried Mya, pointing to the leaves outside of the window. 'They're
dancing again mummy!'
Mya copied the moves of the leaves, waving her hands lightly side to side
and crouching down low, slowly, towards the soft carpet.

She smiled as she did her leaf dance, she knew she must have looked very
funny.
Mya's mum, watching her, let out a loud long laugh. 'Yes they are Mya.
Can you tell me how many dancing leaves you can see?'

Mya stopped dancing and looked outside the window. She tried to count the leaves but there were just too many of them, moving and wiggling.

Mya finally saw five green leaves in a row. She held up one hand with her fingers spread apart, like a small high five and showed her mum.

'Miss Mya, what happened to your voice? Are you giving me a small high five or are you showing me the number of leaves you counted?' asked Mya's mum with a puzzled look. Sometimes Mya's mum could be silly and sometimes Mya could be even sillier.
'Both!' Mya said as she tapped her mum's palm.

'Oh alright cheeky! Come on Mya, let's get ready for Sunday lunch at Grandma and Grandpa's. What colour top do you want to wear today?'

On the bed behind Mya, her mum had hidden three different coloured tops. One was yellow, one was orange and one was green.

'Let's play the guessing game, that always helps you choose a colour,' Mya's
mum said.
'Okay,' Mya said with a smile, 'that's my favourite game to play.'

'Hmmm, one is the same colour as the sun. It's very bright and reminds me of the summer time. It's also the same colour as Daddy's favourite fruit. What colour am I describing Mya?'

Mya took a deep breath and thought of the sun. She thought of summer time fun. She thought of Daddy's favourite fruit. She thought and thought.

'Ohhh I know, it's yellow!' Mya said with a shout as she hopped and jumped about. 'It's got to be yellow because Daddy's favourite fruit is a banana and a banana is yellow. The sun's yellow too.'

Mya's mum waited until Mya settled down. 'Yes Mya, you clever girl. Well done! Are you ready for the next two?' Mya's mum asked.
Mya gave a big nod, sat down on the carpet eagerly and waited.

'Okay,' Mya's mum said, 'the second top is the same colour as a round fruit with the same name. It is also Grandma's favourite colour.'

'The third one is the same colour as the leaves in spring. It's also the same colour as grass, so think of the grass in the park by your school. What two colours am I describing Mya?'

Mya stood still with a finger held against her lips. She thought about all the round fruits with the same name as a colour.
She thought of grandma's favourite colour. Last Christmas, Grandma knitted an orange scarf for Mya and said she loved how bright the colour orange was.

'Mummy, the second top is orange!'
'You're right Mya, smarty pants! Now, what about the last colour I described?'

Mya thought about the spring leaves. She thought about the grass in the park right by her school. Grass is green and so are spring leaves.
'The colour you're describing is green, but you forgot that yucky peas are green too! That would have been a good clue.'

'That's true Mya, peas are green, but remember not everyone finds them yucky and you would have guessed it straight away! Right, pick a colour and let's get ready to go,' said Mya's mum.

'Can I wear the orange one? Because it's granny's favourite colour.'
Mya walked over and stood by the bed, with her arms held above her head,
ready for the top to be tightly pulled over her.

Mya, in her beautiful orange top, walked in between her parents. She skipped and she hopped; skipped, skipped, skipped, hopped, hopped, hopped her way towards Grandma and Grandpa's house.

Her parents laughed. Mya's dad said, with his deep yet soft voice, 'are you sure this is Mya? With all that skipping and hopping, it looks more like we're walking with a bunny.'

Mya stopped and looked at her mum and dad. *They can't really think I'm a bunny*, she thought.

'You're right, I'm not too sure now. I mean it does look like Mya,' Mya's mum said eyeing Mya suspiciously.

Mya let out a laugh

'And sounds a lot like Mya too,' observed her dad.

Mya's mum squeezed and squished Mya's big cheeks.
'It feels like Mya too.'

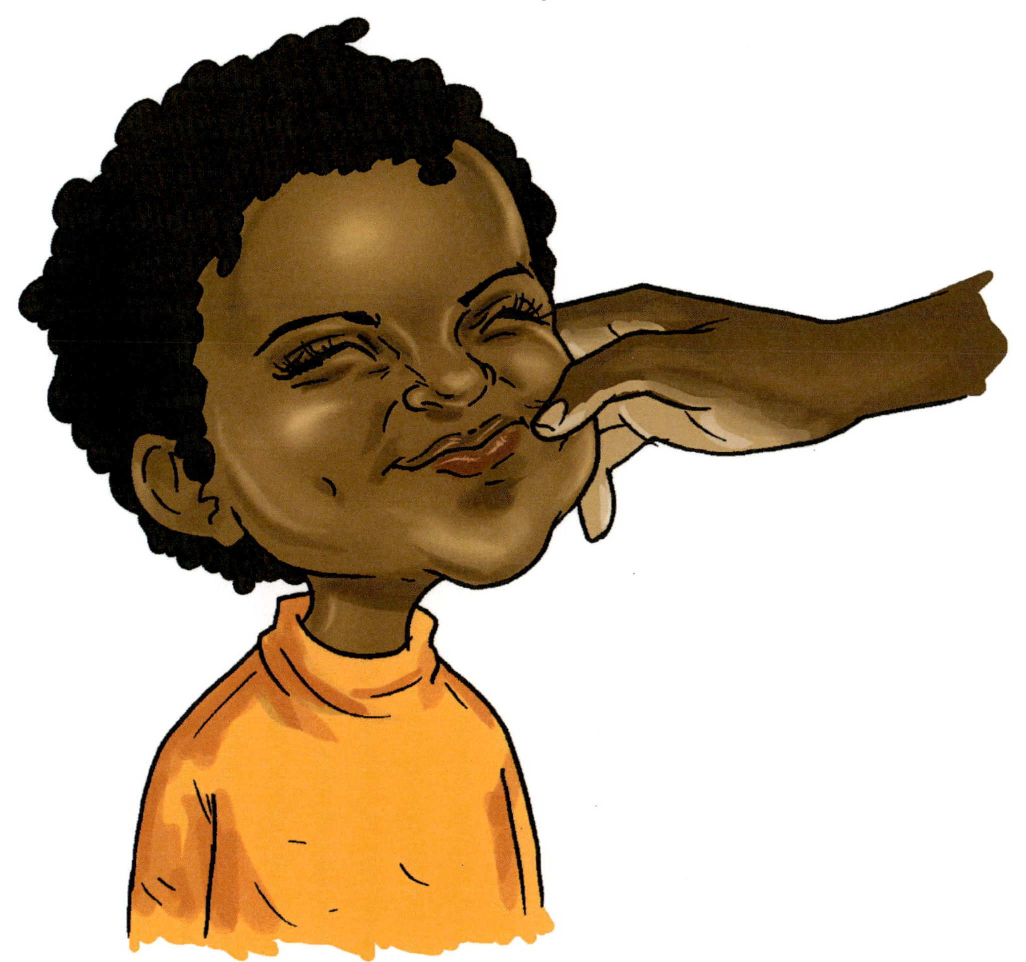

'It is Mya!' Mya yelled.
'Oh! My mistake,' said Mya's dad, 'I am so glad it's Mya and not a bunny.'
'Me too,' said Mya's mum
'Me three,' added Mya, 'come on, let's go.' She grabbed her parents' hands
and pulled them along.

She knew her parents could play pretend forever but Mya was hungry and wanted to eat all of her favourite foods before her cousins arrived at Grandma and Grandpa's.

Mya was a slow eater and her cousins knew this. She often missed out on second helpings. She sometimes even missed out on firsts, as hands would swoop in and snatch things from her plate.
'Next time eat faster' would be the response to her angry cries of 'hey' and 'that's not fair.'

Mya's mum and dad swung Mya up onto the little step in front of her grandparents' door.

'Granny, it's me Myaaaaa.'
Mya's dad coughed and Mya's mum cleared her throat.
'Oh and mummy and daddy too of course.'

When Mya's Granny opened the door Mya could smell the food her grandparents had spent all morning preparing. She closed her eyes and sniffed.

Her nose was filled with the delicious smell of plantain, sweet potatoes, her grandpa's spicy jerk chicken, curry, yams, fried fish, beans, gravy, jollof rice and mac & cheese.

'Hi Mya, I've missed you so much,' Mya's Granny said as she bent down to give Mya a big soft kiss on the cheek.

'I've missed you too, Granny', replied Mya, giving her Granny a warm hug. The sounds of laughter and cheers interrupted Mya's cuddle with her Granny. 'Your cousins are here already,' said Granny, standing up straight. She took a glance at Mya's worried expression.

'Don't worry lunch hasn't been served yet. We were waiting for you to arrive. Everyone is in the front room playing a game with Grandpa.'
Mya's face broke out into a wide grin and she began skipping again, down the hallway, towards the sounds of her waiting family.

Mya loved spending time with her family. She didn't care how loud or quiet they were, or how tall or short they were, how many or few they were. She loved being around each and every member, they were all special to her. That's why Mya loved whenever Sunday lunch was at Grandma and Grandpa's because she got to see everyone together.
She wished she could have these lunches all the time.

At these lunches, she found out about life in big school and how hard it was not to get detention - whatever that was.

She found out about something called drama, which she found confusing. Her cousin Leanne said she loved drama and that acting was fun and exciting but Mya remembered her mum speaking about drama on the phone. Her mum said that drama was bad and should be avoided at all costs.

Her cousins Grace and Leanne lived with Uncle Aaron.
Joseph and baby Reneé lived with Aunty Catherine and Uncle Jeff.
Uncle Kwasi and Aunty Sophie lived together.
Tara and Charlie both went to University so they lived with their friends.

Then there was Mya who lived with her dad, her mum and her favourite teddy named Patchy. Mya chose to call her teddy, 'Patchy' because of the different patches of fabric that was sewn on him.

22

Tara and Charlie spoke about something called a degree. Mya was confused again because they both did degrees but the degrees were different.
Joseph, her dad and Grandpa spoke about football.
Aunty Catherine and Uncle Jeff spoke to Mya's mum about baby Reneé teething.

Uncle Aaron was playing cards with Uncle Kwasi and everyone else had conversations about things Mya couldn't quite hear.

Suddenly, Mya couldn't quite hear anything. Her eyes felt really heavy and she could hardly see even though she really wanted to.

'Aw look at Mya' Grace said gently, 'she's fallen asleep. All that fighting with Joseph over her plantain must have really knocked her out.' Everyone laughed.

Then Grandma picked her up and placed Mya lightly on her and grandpa's bed before covering her with a nice fluffy blanket. The laughter, games and story-telling continued until the evening.
When the sky becomes dark and clear and the stars magically reappear.
When the clouds float away and the night sky takes over the day.

Lightning Source UK Ltd.
Milton Keynes UK
UKRC02n0503251018
331152UK00002BA/40

9780995601758